My First Book of
QUANTUM PHYSICS

Sheddad Kaid-Salah Ferrón & Eduard Altarriba

Button
BOOKS

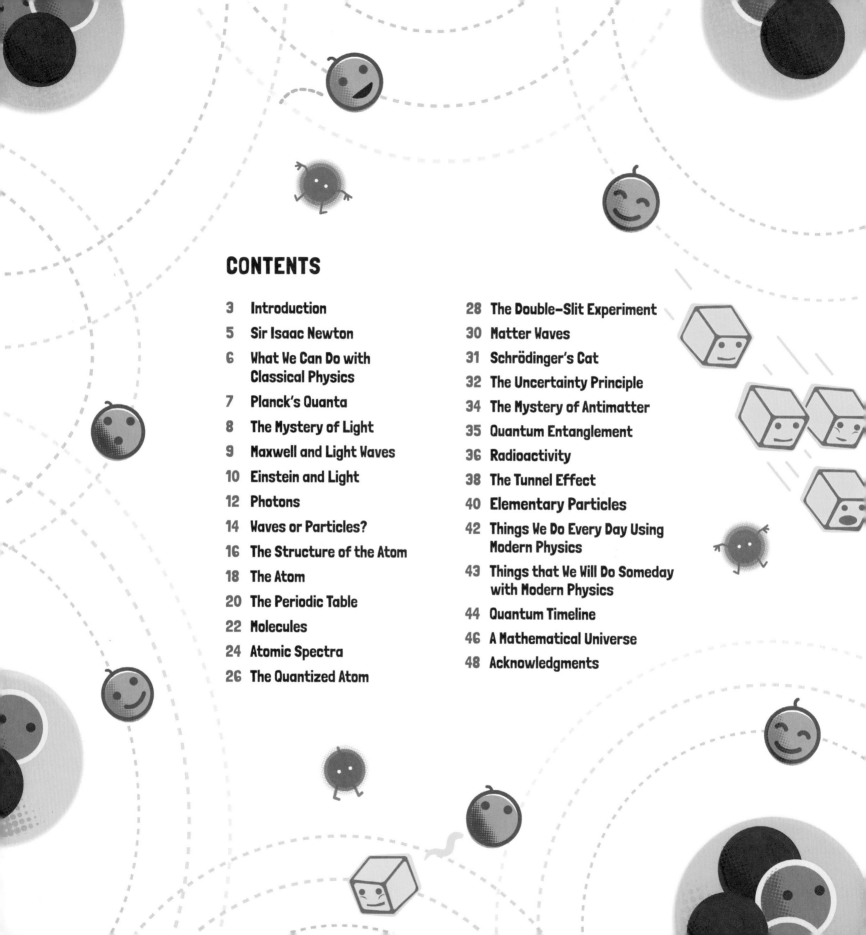

CONTENTS

INTRODUCTION

Everything around us—trees, buildings, food, light, water, air, and even ourselves—is composed of very, very small things known as subatomic particles. When scientists started to discover more about these particles, they realized that in such a tiny world, the laws of physics did not apply. They needed to generate a whole new set of theories, which we know today as quantum physics. This is the science of subatomic particles, and without it none of our electronic devices, from smartphones to computers and microwave ovens, would exist.

But quantum physics remains a mystery for most people, despite the fact that it is part of our daily lives. It pushes us to the very boundaries of what we know about science, reality, and the structure of the universe. The world of quantum physics is an amazing place, where particles can do weird and wonderful things, acting totally unlike the objects we experience in day-to-day life. This book is an introduction to the subject for children aged 8 and above (and their parents). It is obviously not an academic book, but its aim is to introduce key concepts of quantum physics in the easiest and most entertaining way possible.

For centuries, people tried to understand the world from what could be seen and felt. Things that could not be explained in this way, such as the stars or the origin of the world, were explained using myths and religion. For example, even from the top of a mountain, it is very difficult to imagine that the Earth is round or to appreciate the vastness of the universe. In order to reach these conclusions, it was necessary to be daring and to think in a completely different way.

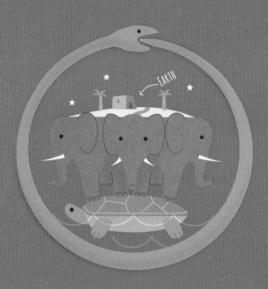

Most civilizations believed in gods whom they thought had created the world. In Hindu mythology the Earth is held up by four elephants, which are supported by a tortoise that rests on a snake that eats its tail. For many centuries, most people in Europe were convinced that the Earth was flat.

The ancient Greek philosophers were among the first to suspect that our senses were not enough to understand the world, and that we needed observation, experimentation, and mathematics too. In the 2nd century BCE, Eratosthenes was already able to calculate the circumference of the Earth, and centuries later the Arab scholars Al-Farghani and Al-Biruni would do the same.

At the end of the Middle Ages, the idea that the Earth was actually round or spherical started to take hold. Most people still believed that the Earth was the center of the universe and that the Sun revolved around it. But in the 16th century the mathematician and astronomer Nicolaus Copernicus made observations using astronomical instruments to study the sky. His model placed the Sun at the center of our planetary system.

Sir Isaac
NEWTON

From the 16th century onward, we started to understand the world through science, thanks to people such as Galileo Galilei and Sir Isaac Newton.

Why does an apple fall from the tree? Everybody knows that things fall to the ground, but Sir Isaac Newton (1643–1727) was the first to answer this question in a scientific way. Based on observations and calculations, he came up with the Law of Universal Gravitation, which explained, for example, why things fall to the ground, why the Moon revolves around the Earth, and why the planets orbit around the Sun. He also established the Three Laws of Motion (also known as Newton's laws), which explain how and why things move. These laws can be used to calculate the path of a billiard ball or to know the force or strength that is needed to kick a ball toward the opposing goal line.

WHAT WE CAN DO WITH CLASSICAL PHYSICS

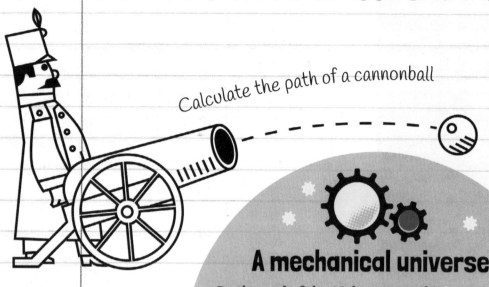

Calculate the path of a cannonball

Calculate the path of a space rocket

A mechanical universe

By the end of the 19th century the laws of nature, discovered by scientists such as Sir Isaac Newton, were able to explain most of the phenomena that occur in our world through mathematics.

These laws (or theories) are part of what we know as classical physics. Thanks to these laws, major breakthroughs were made in fields such as engineering, industry, and astronomy. It seemed that scientists had studied and calculated almost everything, but not everything can be explained using classical physics...

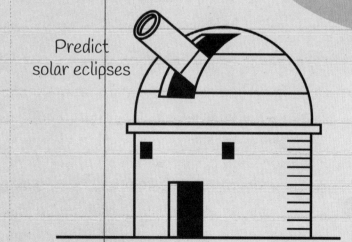

Predict solar eclipses

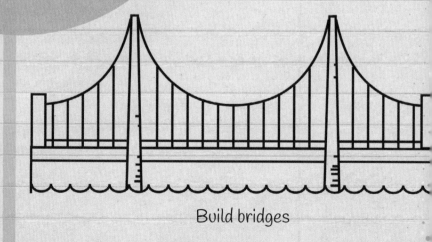

Build bridges

The problem started with **PLANCK's** famous **QUANTA**

A piece of cold metal does not emit light. If we start to heat it, we will see that it still does not emit any light. But if we continue to gradually heat the metal, it will start to glow until it becomes red-hot and if we heat it a lot, it will even emit WHITE LIGHT.

The scientist Max Planck wanted to find the relationship between the light emitted by a hot object and its temperature.

After giving it a lot of thought, the only way that Planck found to tally the numbers with his observations of the experiments was to divide the energy that the hot object emitted into very small packets which he called QUANTA (the singular is "quantum").

QUANTA are packets of ENERGY. They are INDIVISIBLE, which means we cannot divide them into smaller pieces.

PLANCK EXPLAINED WHY OBJECTS EMIT LIGHT WHEN THEY ARE HEATED.

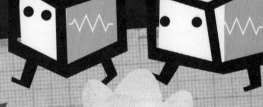

A small quantity of quanta

Energy

We all know what energy is, but trying to describe it is not so easy. In physics, energy is defined as the ability to do work.

Energy CANNOT be created or destroyed; it can only be transformed, in one way or another.

According to classical physics, energy is CONTINUOUS—we can divide it into as many little pieces as we wish. However, since Planck's quanta were INDIVISIBLE, they did not fit in with that idea at all.

QUANTA WERE THE FIRST INDICATION THAT THINGS ACTUALLY WORK ACCORDING TO LAWS THAT ARE WAY BEYOND THE HUMAN SCALE. A DIFFERENT WAY OF THINKING WAS NEEDED.

But first of all we have to go back in time to talk about

the Mystery of LIGHT

WAVE or PARTICLE?

Even back in Newton's time, a debate was going on about whether light was made up of particles or waves. For Newton, light was formed by tiny PARTICLES (which he called corpuscles) that moved in a straight line.

← Newtonian corpuscles travelling in a straight line

On the other hand, many others believed that light had to be formed by WAVES because otherwise they would not be able to explain the DIFFRACTION of light, a phenomenon that causes light to change direction.

LIGHT PHENOMENA

REFLECTION is the phenomenon that occurs when light bounces off a surface, such as when we look at ourselves in a mirror.

DIFFRACTION is the capability of light to change direction when finding an obstacle or crossing a slit.

REFRACTION is the phenomenon that occurs when light changes direction as it moves from one medium to another. This is why a pencil appears to be crooked when it is placed in a glass that is full of water.

WHAT IS A PARTICLE?

A PARTICLE is a very small portion of matter.

For example, grains of sand are beach particles. As we will see, everything is made up of very small particles called atoms.

MAXWELL and LIGHT WAVES

Toward the end of the 19th century, James Clerk Maxwell realized that the behavior of light could be explained in mathematical terms, and he described it as if it were formed by WAVES. But WAVES OF WHAT?

Well, the answer is waves of electricity and magnetism: in other words, ELECTROMAGNETIC waves.

LIGHT IS A WAVE

MAXWELL DEVELOPED FOUR FAMOUS EQUATIONS TO DESCRIBE ALL THE ELECTROMAGNETIC PHENOMENA.

WHAT IS A WAVE?

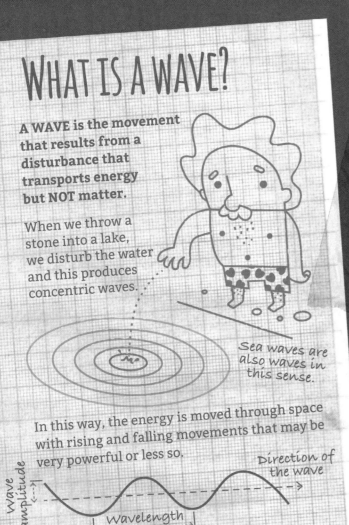

A WAVE is the movement that results from a disturbance that transports energy but NOT matter.

When we throw a stone into a lake, we disturb the water and this produces concentric waves.

Sea waves are also waves in this sense.

In this way, the energy is moved through space with rising and falling movements that may be very powerful or less so.

Wave amplitude

Direction of the wave

Wavelength

Light moves at an incredible speed:

This is the speed of LIGHT! 300,000 km per second

At this speed, it would be possible to go around the Earth seven and a half times in just one second.

TRY TO IMAGINE THE ENORMOUS LENGTH OF A LIGHT YEAR, WHICH IS THE DISTANCE THAT LIGHT TRAVELS IN ONE EARTH YEAR!

This is how Maxwell got around the old "wave or particle" conflict, and he decided in favor of the notion of light behaving as a wave.

It seemed that the problem had been resolved, but then things got a bit complicated...

EINSTEIN and LIGHT

IN 1900, PHYSICISTS WERE FACED WITH ANOTHER UNSOLVED PROBLEM.

This was the PHOTOELECTRIC[1] effect, which allows us to transform light into electricity.

[1] "Photo" means "light" in classical Greek.

But what exactly is electricity?

Electrons are negatively charged particles that form a part of all atoms (we will talk about atoms later).

An electric current is the movement of electrons within matter.

What does the PHOTOELECTRIC effect consist of?

If we make an electric circuit using a light bulb and two pieces of metal, and then light up the metal with a VIOLET light, we will see that the bulb also lights up.

This happens because the electrons jump from one piece of metal to the other, and this allows the electric current to circulate.

But if we do the same with a RED light, we find that the electrons do NOT jump and the electric current does not circulate, and naturally enough, the bulb does not light up.

So why do we have light in one case but not in the other?

Using Planck's ideas about quanta, Albert EINSTEIN realized that if light, rather than being formed by waves, consisted of particles (which he called PHOTONS), it would be possible to explain the photoelectric effect in the following way:

Today, we use this photoelectric effect in many devices for a variety of uses. One example is the sensors in the automatic doors of elevators or stores. It is also used to create electricity in solar panels.

If we light up the metal with VIOLET light, the VIOLET PHOTONS collide with the electrons of the metal and knock them out one by one.

RED PHOTONS, on the other hand, do not have enough energy to knock the electrons from the metal, and no matter how many photons we send, they will not be able to do it.

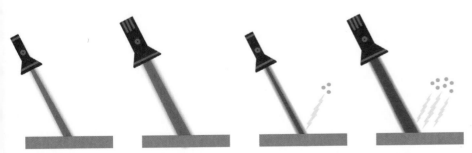

Photons are the elementary particles that make up light

Photons are also known as LIGHT QUANTA, or ENERGY QUANTA as Einstein liked to call them.

They are very special particles as they have no mass, are indivisible, and travel at the SPEED of LIGHT (see page 9).

PHOTONS

PARTICLES OF LIGHT

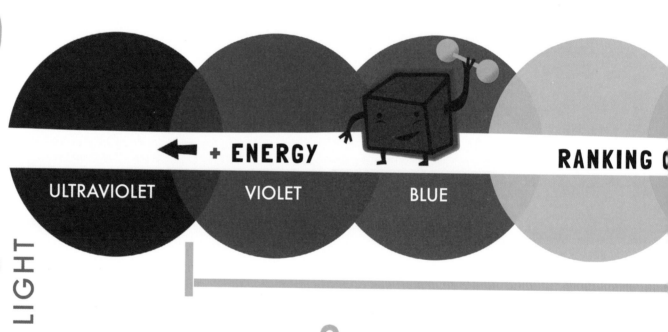

← + ENERGY

ULTRAVIOLET   VIOLET   BLUE   RANKING O

FREQUENCY

The color of light is determined by its FREQUENCY—the number of waves that pass a given point per second.

Depending on the color of the light, we will have one type of photon or another. We can have blue, green, yellow, red photons, etc.

The higher the frequency of a photon, the more energy it will have.

The frequency of blue light is greater than the frequency of red light and therefore BLUE photons will have more energy than RED photons.

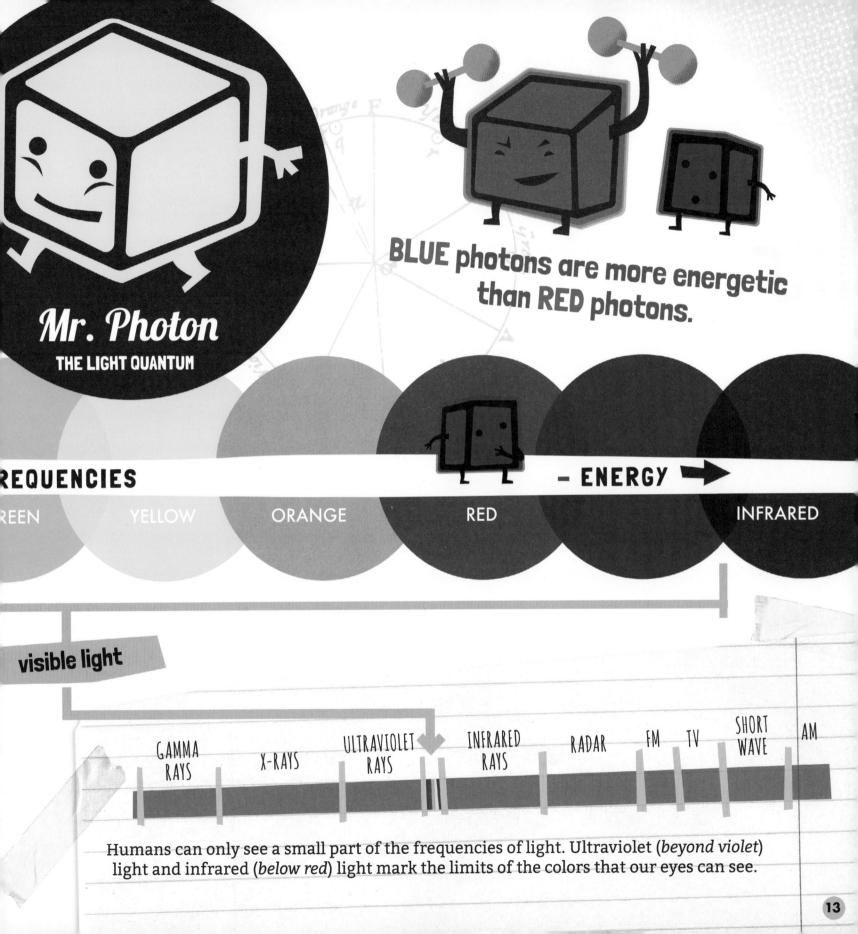

Mr. Photon
THE LIGHT QUANTUM

BLUE photons are more energetic than RED photons.

FREQUENCIES — ENERGY →

GREEN • YELLOW • ORANGE • RED • INFRARED

visible light

GAMMA RAYS • X-RAYS • ULTRAVIOLET RAYS • INFRARED RAYS • RADAR • FM • TV • SHORT WAVE • AM

Humans can only see a small part of the frequencies of light. Ultraviolet (*beyond violet*) light and infrared (*below red*) light mark the limits of the colors that our eyes can see.

WAVES OR PARTICLES?

The dilemma...

Thinking of light as a wave allows us to explain phenomena such as diffraction. (Maxwell)

The photoelectric effect and other phenomena of light can only be explained if we think that light is formed by particles. (Newton and Einstein)

Finally, there are phenomena that can be explained using both theories, for example, how light travels in a straight line (reflection and refraction).

It looks as though there are two contradictory images of reality. Taken separately, neither of them fully explains the phenomena of light, whereas TOGETHER, THEY DO.
(Albert Einstein)

We must accept the fact that light sometimes behaves like a wave while at other times it behaves like a particle.

Strange, isn't it? So then, what causes it to behave one way or the other?

Well, this actually depends on how we are observing things. In other words, it depends on the type of experiment that we are carrying out.

GIVE ME A HIGH-FIVE, PHOTON.

WHAT A WAVE!

THE STRANGE BEHAVIOR OF LIGHT DID NOT FIT IN WITH THE OLD LAWS OF PHYSICS. THAT IS HOW QUANTUM THEORY STARTED.

This very unusual behavior of light is called the
WAVE–PARTICLE DUALITY.

But the most incredible thing is that light particles aren't the only ones to behave like this; other particles also show wave–particle duality. We will see this later on.

Imagine cutting a cake into pieces

We can start by cutting the cake in half, and we can then divide the halves in half, and then cut these halves in half and so on... but how long can we keep cutting?

DEMOCRITUS CUTTING A CAKE

AFTER THE GREEKS, 2,000 YEARS WOULD GO BY BEFORE PHYSICISTS DISCOVERED THE ATOM.

Back in ancient Greece, about 2,500 years ago, people wondered what matter was made of.

Some philosophers thought that it was possible to keep cutting things into smaller pieces for as long as we liked.

There were others, such as Democritus, who thought that there came a moment when matter could not be divided any further. In other words, that it was formed by indivisible particles, which they called ATOMS (in Greek, "atom" means "indivisible," or "which cannot be divided.")

In 1909, Ernest RUTHERFORD carried out a famous experiment that revealed the structure of the atom.

He and his collaborators fired some ALPHA particles, as if they were bullets, against a very fine piece of gold foil to see what happened.

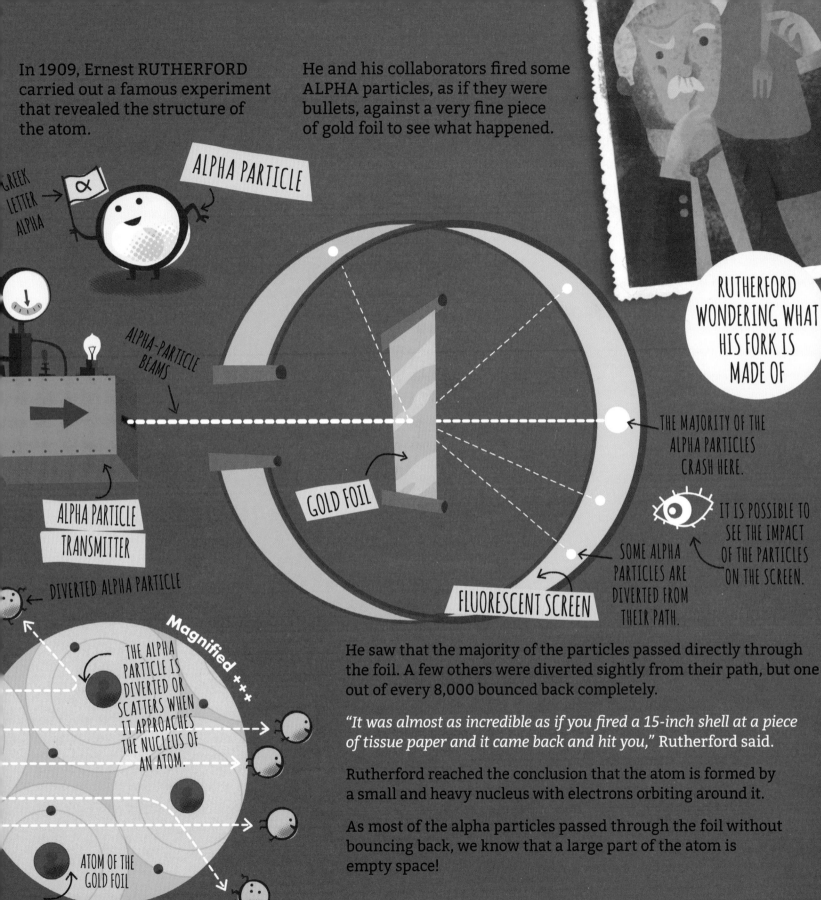

GREEK LETTER ALPHA →

ALPHA PARTICLE

ALPHA-PARTICLE BEAMS

ALPHA PARTICLE TRANSMITTER

GOLD FOIL

RUTHERFORD WONDERING WHAT HIS FORK IS MADE OF

THE MAJORITY OF THE ALPHA PARTICLES CRASH HERE.

IT IS POSSIBLE TO SEE THE IMPACT OF THE PARTICLES ON THE SCREEN.

SOME ALPHA PARTICLES ARE DIVERTED FROM THEIR PATH.

FLUORESCENT SCREEN

DIVERTED ALPHA PARTICLE

Magnified +++

THE ALPHA PARTICLE IS DIVERTED OR SCATTERS WHEN IT APPROACHES THE NUCLEUS OF AN ATOM.

ATOM OF THE GOLD FOIL

He saw that the majority of the particles passed directly through the foil. A few others were diverted sightly from their path, but one out of every 8,000 bounced back completely.

"It was almost as incredible as if you fired a 15-inch shell at a piece of tissue paper and it came back and hit you," Rutherford said.

Rutherford reached the conclusion that the atom is formed by a small and heavy nucleus with electrons orbiting around it.

As most of the alpha particles passed through the foil without bouncing back, we know that a large part of the atom is empty space!

THE ATOM

All matter is made up of ATOMS, and atoms, in turn, are also formed by different particles: electrons, protons, and neutrons.

ELECTRONS are scattered around the nucleus, forming clouds that we call **ORBITALS**.

In an atom there are as many electrons as protons in the nucleus.

The **NUCLEUS** is formed by neutrons and protons.

The force that unites protons and neutrons in the nucleus is called the **STRONG NUCLEAR FORCE**.

The protons of the nucleus attract the electrons through **ELECTROMAGNETIC FORCE**.

When an electron receives or emits energy, it can pass from one orbital to another.

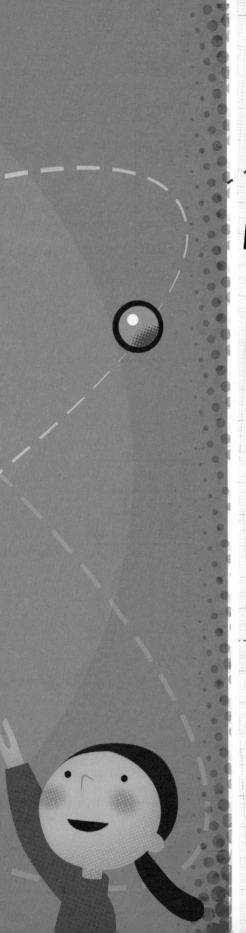

ELECTRON

It is small and has a **negative** electric charge.

NUCLEUS

PROTON

It has a **positive** electric charge.

NEUTRON

It has no electric charge. It is **neutral**.

A more accurate vision of the atom would be something like this:

NUCLEUS

THE ORBITALS FORM A CLOUD AND THEY ARE THE AREAS WHERE THERE IS A GREATER PROBABILITY OF FINDING ELECTRONS.

Until quite recently, it was believed that protons and neutrons were indivisible particles. Now we know that they are made up of other even tinier particles known as QUARKS.

Goodness...

WE ARE EMPTY!

Even though we draw atoms in this way to understand them, their proportions are very different in real terms. If the nucleus were the size of a ball, the electrons would be several kilometers away!

The greater part of an atom is empty space, and since we are made of atoms, this means that...

... WE ARE HOLLOW!

EVERYTHING IS MADE OF ATOMS!

Atoms are the building blocks of our world. By joining different pieces, you can make glass, a piece of wood, the paper of this book, the air that you breathe, your pet, YOUR FRIENDS, YOUR PARENTS, AND YOURSELF!

All atoms have the same particles (protons, neutrons, and electrons), but what makes them different is the number of protons that the nucleus contains.

Different types of atoms make up the ELEMENTS. A HYDROGEN atom, which is the lightest element, only has one proton in its nucleus. On the other hand, URANIUM, which is one of the heaviest elements, contains 92 protons in its nucleus.

We already know of 118 different elements And we keep finding more...

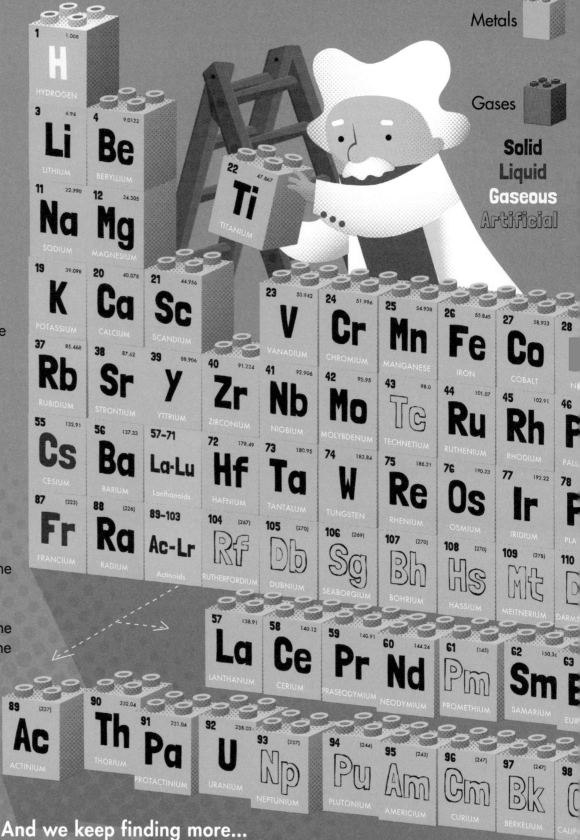

Metals

Gases

Solid
Liquid
Gaseous
Artificial

Non-metals

Metalloids

THE PERIODIC TABLE

Some elements are heavy while others are light. There are soft elements and hard ones. At room temperature some are gaseous, others liquid, while others are solid. Some are metals and others are not. Each element is unique and has its own characteristics.

In 1869, Dmitri MENDELEEV organized the elements in a special way which he called the PERIODIC TABLE. In this table, the elements are ordered according to a growing number of protons in the nucleus and placed in such a way so that those that have similar properties are in the same column.

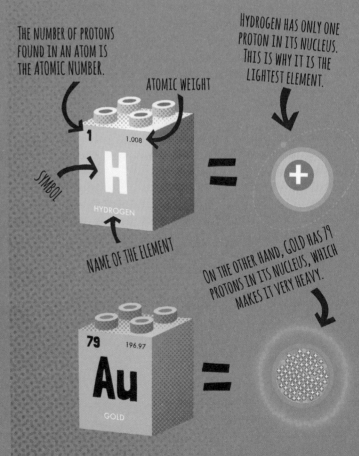

THE NUMBER OF PROTONS FOUND IN AN ATOM IS THE ATOMIC NUMBER.

HYDROGEN HAS ONLY ONE PROTON IN ITS NUCLEUS. THIS IS WHY IT IS THE LIGHTEST ELEMENT.

ATOMIC WEIGHT

SYMBOL

NAME OF THE ELEMENT

ON THE OTHER HAND, GOLD HAS 79 PROTONS IN ITS NUCLEUS, WHICH MAKES IT VERY HEAVY.

REMEMBER THAT THERE ARE AS MANY ELECTRONS IN AN ATOM AS THERE ARE PROTONS IN THE NUCLEUS.

MOLECULES

By combining the atoms of the different elements of the Periodic Table, we get all the substances that we can find in nature.

Most of these substances are groups of atoms called **MOLECULES.**

The atoms that make up each molecule are kept together thanks to the fact that they lose, gain, or share some special electrons known as **VALENCE ELECTRONS.**

THE OXYGEN THAT WE BREATHE IS A MOLECULE FORMED BY ONLY TWO ATOMS OF OXYGEN.

WATER

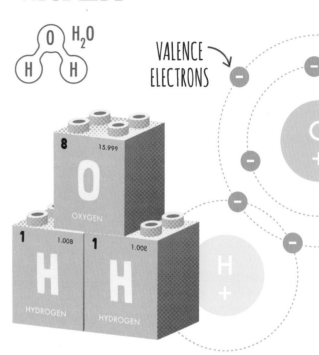

VALENCE ELECTRONS

OZONE

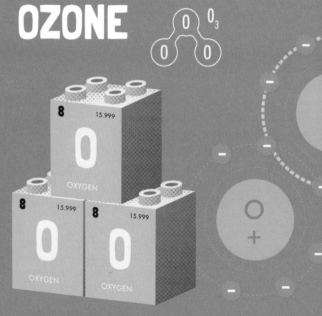

If we join three atoms of oxygen, we get OZONE, which is a very, very toxic gas that is violet in color.

If we combine one atom of oxygen with two atoms of hydrogen we get a MOLECULE of WATER.

However, water is no more than a lot of water molecules grouped together.

In a single one-milliliter drop, there are approximately 33,428,852,150,000,000,000,000 molecules of water.

GLUCOSE

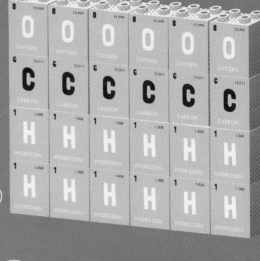

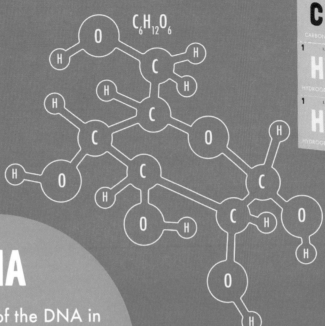

$C_6H_{12}O_6$

The molecule of GLUCOSE is bigger; it has a total of 24 atoms: 6 atoms of carbon, 12 of hydrogen, and 6 of oxygen.

DNA

The molecules of the DNA in our cells are among the largest that there are. They can have millions of atoms!

THE SHARED ELECTRONS ARE ALWAYS IN THE OUTER LAYERS, THOSE FARTHEST FROM THE NUCLEUS.

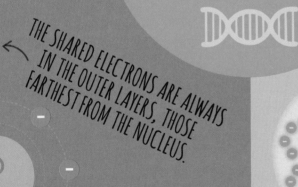

Fe 2+

Fe 2+

Fe 2+

Fe 2+

ELECTRON CLOUD

IRON

26   55.845

Fe

IRON

Metals are a special case. We can think of them as a super molecule formed by lots of metal atoms that share all their valence electrons: a CLOUD of ELECTRONS that can travel freely.

ATOMIC SPECTRA

When we heat an atomic element into a gaseous state, it emits LIGHT.

When we break this light down with a prism, unlike **sunlight**, we do not get all the colors. We only see a few lines of different colors.

This is the element's EMISSION SPECTRUM.

Each element of the Periodic Table has its own **spectrum** and it is different from those of the other elements.

For example, the **spectrum** of oxygen is different from the spectrum of hydrogen.

HYDROGEN EMISSION SPECTRUM

LIGHT SPECTRUM

OXYGEN EMISSION SPECTRUM

If we break down the light of a **star** and the spectrum of the **hydrogen** element appears, we will know that there are **hydrogen** atoms in it. This way, we can find out what elements the stars contain even though we cannot reach them.

To obtain the spectrum of the light of a star, we use a device called a SPECTROSCOPE. This instrument is very sensitive and precise, but essentially, it does the same work as a prism: it breaks the light down.

At the beginning of the 20th century, physicists had discovered the spectra of many elements of the Periodic Table but they didn't know how to explain them.

IT WAS THE DANISH PHYSICIST NIELS BOHR WHO FOUND THE SOLUTION.

NIELS BOHR

THE DANISH PHYSICIST NIELS BOHR WONDERING WHAT ATOMS ARE

BOHR came up with a great idea to explain emission spectra and other phenomena of the atom.

He thought that the electrons in the atom move in orbits around the nucleus just as the planets go around the Sun. But there was one difference: they can only occupy SPECIAL orbits where they feel "comfortable."

All other orbits are forbidden to them. These special orbits are said to be QUANTIZED.

1

1. THE ELECTRON CIRCULATES IN A LEISURELY MANNER THROUGH THE ORBIT IN WHICH IT FEELS "COMFORTABLE."

Th

ELECTRON

THE REL
PHOTON

4

4. IN ORDER TO GO BACK DOWN TO THE ORBIT WHERE IT WAS BEFORE, IT SHEDS THE ABSORBED ENERGY BY RELEASING A PHOTON.

ALL THE RELEASED PHOTONS ARE OF THE SAME COLOR

Quantized Atom

(according to Bohr)

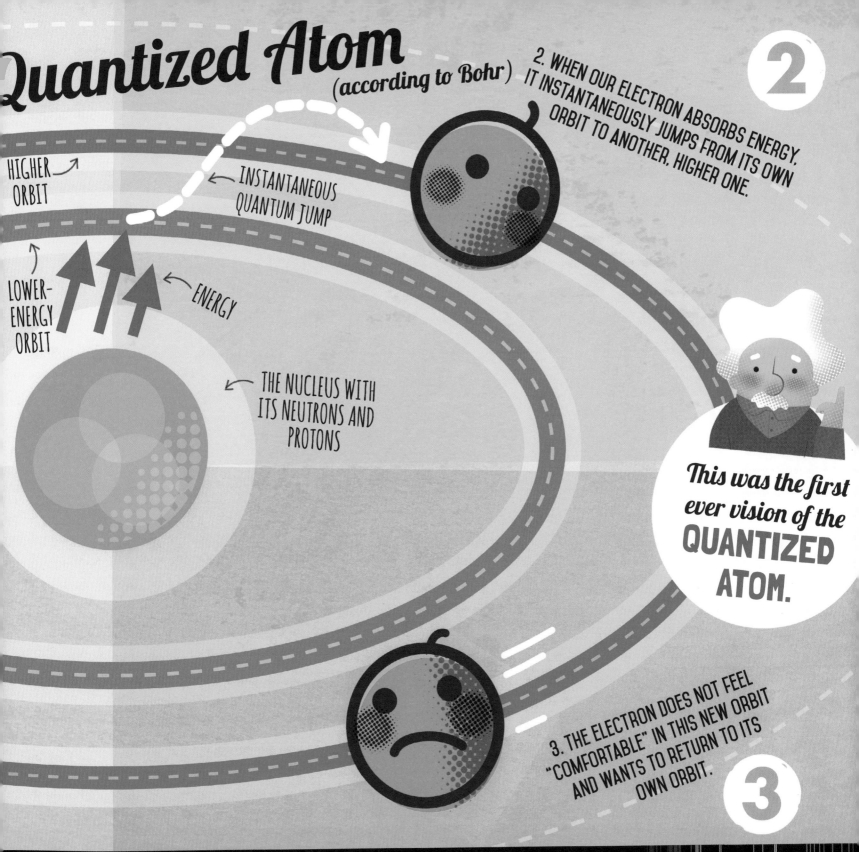

2. WHEN OUR ELECTRON ABSORBS ENERGY, IT INSTANTANEOUSLY JUMPS FROM ITS OWN ORBIT TO ANOTHER, HIGHER ONE.

HIGHER ORBIT

INSTANTANEOUS QUANTUM JUMP

LOWER-ENERGY ORBIT

ENERGY

THE NUCLEUS WITH ITS NEUTRONS AND PROTONS

This was the first ever vision of the **QUANTIZED ATOM.**

3. THE ELECTRON DOES NOT FEEL "COMFORTABLE" IN THIS NEW ORBIT AND WANTS TO RETURN TO ITS OWN ORBIT.

3

(SAME FREQUENCY) AND THESE ARE THE ONES THAT WE SEE IN THE LINES OF THE EMISSION SPECTRA.

THE DOUBLE-SLIT

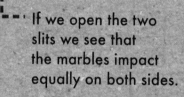

This famous experiment showed us that subatomic particles behave in an incredible way.

To begin, imagine we have a gun that shoots marbles and another that shoots waves. We are going to fire at a wall that has two slits.

1 Firing Marbles

If we shoot marbles with only one slit open, we will see that almost all of the marbles impact opposite the slit that we have left open.

If we open the two slits we see that the marbles impact equally on both sides.

PATTERN OF THE PARTICLES

2 Firing Waves

If we fire waves against the two slits, what we get is a WAVE pattern (bet you guessed that!) This is easier to understand by drawing it.

WAVE (OR INTERFERENCE) PATTERN

In 1801, Thomas Young was the first person to do this experiment with light. This allowed him to see that light behaved like a wave. But, a wave of what? As we have already seen, Maxwell described light as an ELECTROMAGNETIC WAVE (a wave of electricity and magnetism).

EXPERIMENT

Up to now everything has been quite normal, hasn't it? But what happens if we go to the subatomic world? We are going to do the double-slit experiment with **electrons**.

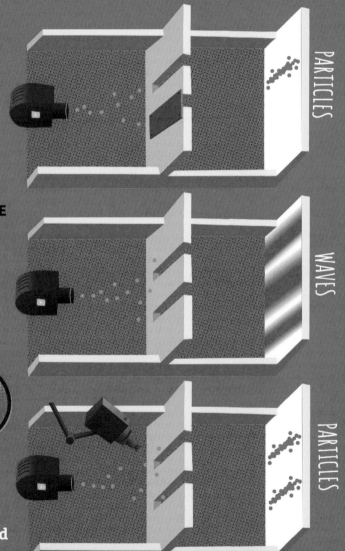

① With one of the slits covered

If we fire electrons with one of the two slits closed, we see that the electrons behave like the marbles. We get a **pattern of PARTICLES** on the screen.

② With both slits open

This is where the amazing stuff begins, because in this case we get a **WAVE pattern**. The electrons do not behave like particles but **like WAVES**.

⁉ And how do the electrons know if the two slits are open, or if only one is open? Do they warn each other and decide to behave either as a WAVE or as a PARTICLE? Do they first pass through one and then through the other before reaching the detector, and is that how they know what to do?

③ What if we observe what happens?

Scientists placed an instrument to "see" what side the electrons passed on when the two slits were open, but then the electrons started to behave **like PARTICLES again**.

⁉ Do the electrons know that they are being observed and does this cause them to act in one way or the other?

We will answer all these questions by accepting that the electrons are not one thing or the other. Depending on the experiment, they will behave in one way or the other. This is what is known as THE WAVE–PARTICLE DUALITY.

We have already seen that light also behaves in this strange way.

However, it is not only electrons and photons that have this duality. All other subatomic particles, such as protons and neutrons, and even atoms, also behave in this way. And it has even been shown that some large molecules also display this dual behavior!

MATTER WAVES

With the double-slit experiment, we have seen that electrons sometimes behave like waves, but WAVES OF WHAT? We know that they are not waves like LIGHT waves (electromagnetic waves) and neither are they like the waves of a guitar string (mechanical waves).

The French physicist Louis de BROGLIE, inspired by Einstein's light quanta, thought that perhaps matter (electrons) could act like a WAVE.

Very few people took him seriously. However, one physicist, the Austrian Erwin SCHRÖDINGER, did and he looked for a wave equation that could describe matter.

He came to a surprising conclusion:

"Matter waves" are
PROBABILITY WAVES

And... what does that mean?

Let's look at an example:

QUANTUM SPIN

SPIN is a quantum property that particles have. It tells us the direction in which they spin. In the case of an electron, we can only have one of TWO possible states of spin: spin UP (spins to the right) or spin DOWN (spins to the left).

STATE Ⓐ
SPIN UP ELECTRON

STATE Ⓑ
SPIN DOWN ELECTRON

We cannot know at a given moment whether the spin will be up or down. We only know that there is a 50 percent probability that it will be in one state or the other.

STATE Ⓐ

STATE Ⓑ

It is only when we measure the state of the electron with an instrument that we can know whether the spin is UP or DOWN. Then we say that reality COLLAPSES.

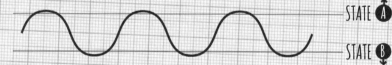
Let's see how Schrödinger used his famous CAT to explain this curious idea.

This is a famous thought experiment (nobody ever put a cat in a box!) that Schrödinger devised in order to explain quantum physics in a simple way.

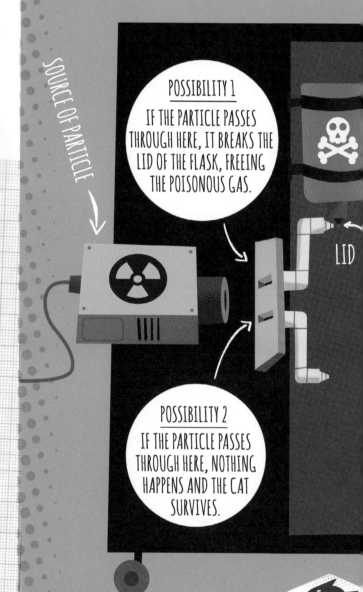

SOURCE OF PARTICLE

POSSIBILITY 1

IF THE PARTICLE PASSES THROUGH HERE, IT BREAKS THE LID OF THE FLASK, FREEING THE POISONOUS GAS.

LID

POSSIBILITY 2

IF THE PARTICLE PASSES THROUGH HERE, NOTHING HAPPENS AND THE CAT SURVIVES.

SCHRÖDINGER'S CAT

Collapsing reality

GATE

ASK OF POISON

CAT

In this experiment, a cat is placed in a box with a flask containing a poisonous gas. Using a mechanism activated by a radioactive particle, the flask has a 50 percent chance of breaking and a 50 percent chance of not breaking.

Until we look inside the box, there is a 50 percent probability that the cat is alive and a 50 percent probability that it is dead.

With the box closed, we can say that the cat is alive and dead at the same time.

It is only when we open the box that we discover the actual state of the cat: it will be either dead or alive but not both at the same time.

When we look, reality collapses, and only then do we know whether the cat is dead or alive.

The **MIND-BLOWING** thing is that it is our act of looking that forces nature to decide what state the cat is in!

Einstein did not like the idea of quantum physics working on the basis of probabilities rather than specific and predictable results. "God doesn't play dice," he said, to express his displeasure.

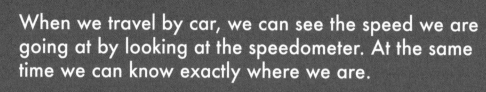

HEISENBERG: THE UNCERTAINTY

When we travel by car, we can see the speed we are going at by looking at the speedometer. At the same time we can know exactly where we are.

In other words, we can know with great accuracy the position and speed of an object at a given moment.

But what happens if we want to know the position and the speed of, let's say, an electron?

The physicist Werner HEISENBERG noticed—as is almost always the case—that things are somewhat different in the quantum world, and he came up with his famous UNCERTAINTY PRINCIPLE (or indeterminacy principle, as he liked to call it):

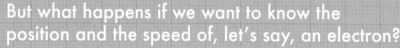

"It is not possible to know with total precision the position and speed of a subatomic particle such as, for example, an electron, at a given moment."

If we know where the electron is, we cannot know its speed and vice versa, if we know its speed, we cannot know where it is...

We can only be 100 percent certain about one parameter at a time—speed or position.

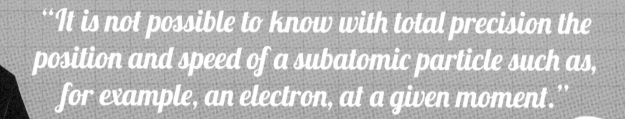

POSITION

SPEED

PRINCIPLE

YOU CHANGE WHAT YOU LOOK AT

If we take a special microscope and use a photon to look at an electron, both of them will collide. We will then have changed the position of the electron, or we will have added or taken away a little speed from it.

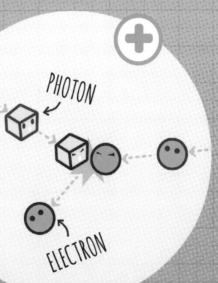

PHOTON

ELECTRON

PHOTON

No matter how good or accurate our measuring device is, things are so small in the quantum world that we cannot avoid disturbing them when we look at them.

The uncertainty principle is also valid in the macroscopic world—what happens there is that objects are so big that it is barely noticeable.

THE MYSTERY OF ANTIMATTER

As we have seen, the MATTER that we know is made up of electrons, protons, and neutrons, which are the PARTICLES that form atoms.

HYDROGEN ATOM
MADE OF MATTER

HYDROGEN ATOM MADE
OF ANTIMATTER

ANTIPARTICLES

The renowned physicist Paul DIRAC predicted that the electron must have a twin particle but with an opposite charge: this is the antielectron or POSITRON. This particle has the same properties as the electron but with a POSITIVE charge. It is the ANTIPARTICLE of the electron.

The same thing happens with the proton; it has its antiparticle, the ANTIPROTON: a proton with a negative charge.

In general terms, all the particles that we know have an antiparticle.

ANTIMATTER

A hydrogen atom is made of one proton and one electron (it's the only atom that doesn't have a neutron).

We can create an ANTIATOM of hydrogen by joining an ANTIPROTON and a POSITRON.

ANTIMATTER atoms can be created using ANTIPARTICLES.

What happens when an ELECTRON and a POSITRON come together? Well, they mutually destroy each other, generating a pair of GAMMA rays (see page 36).

BE VERY CAREFUL IF YOU EVER
MEET YOUR ANTI-ME: DO NOT
SHAKE ITS HAND! THE EXPLOSION
WOULD BE COLOSSAL.

Don't worry. Antimatter is very rare in our universe. We do not know why so little of it exists. Even though there are several theories that have tried to explain this imbalance, it is still an unresolved mystery in physics.

QUANTUM ENTANGLEMENT

In quantum mechanics it is possible to have a series of particles that interact in such a way that they behave as a single system. It is said that they are entangled.

Whatever the distance between them, what happens to one particle will affect the others.

In the laboratory we can "create" a quantum system with two entangled photons in such a way that one of them has SPIN UP and the other SPIN DOWN.

We do not know which spin each one has. It is RANDOM. If we measure the spin in one of the photons and we get UP, when we measure the other one, we will automatically get spin DOWN.

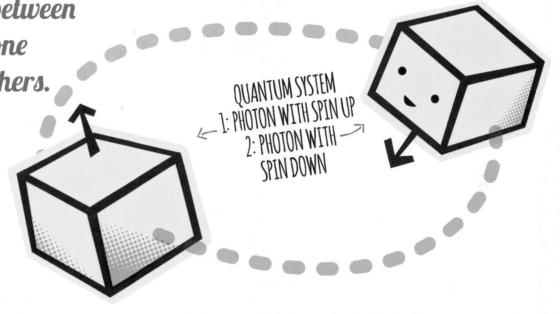

QUANTUM SYSTEM
1: PHOTON WITH SPIN UP
2: PHOTON WITH SPIN DOWN

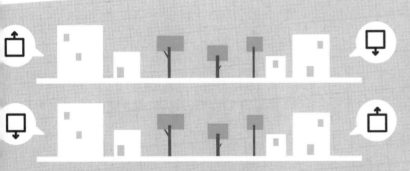

The photons communicate with each other at a distance, as if they were speaking to one other in an INSTANTANEOUS way: "Hey, I've got UP this time, so now it's your turn to be DOWN."

The incredible thing is that it does not matter how far one is from the other. If one is on Earth and the other on Mars, the exact same thing will happen!

How is it possible that they communicate with each other instantaneously, regardless of how far apart they are, if one of the laws of the universe is that nothing can go **faster than the speed of light?**

This is what Einstein referred to as a SPOOKY ACTION AT A DISTANCE.

This is part of the strangeness of the quantum world. Many scientists do NOT like this idea, but it would seem that this is how the world is.

This has been proven many times in the laboratory through a test devised by the physicist John BELL.

RADIOACTIVITY

Henri BECQUEREL discovered natural radioactivity in 1896. He found that certain minerals that contained uranium, such as pitchblende (a strange name, isn't it?), emitted radiation spontaneously.

What does it consist of?

Some atoms have such a big nucleus that they start to feel "UNCOMFORTABLE." In order to **reduce their mass, they get rid of some pieces and release them in the form of radiation.**

They do this SPONTANEOUSLY, and they can do it in three different ways:

ALPHA Radiation (α)

The nucleus of the atom suddenly releases two excess neutrons and two excess protons in the form of a positively charged helium nucleus.

GAMMA Radiation (γ)

In this case, the nucleus emits high-energy photons to get rid of some of the energy that it does not need.

BETA Radiation (β⁻)

The nucleus transforms a neutron into a proton, and it also emits an electron, which is the radiation that we detect.

A curious thing: in certain cases, the opposite happens—a proton becomes a neutron and it emits a POSITRON. CAREFUL! ANTIMATTER is created. This is BETA PLUS radiation (β⁺).

In all cases, the atoms get rid of a little energy so as to feel more "COMFORTABLE."

Remember that this getting rid of energy also happens with ORBITAL electrons when they jump from a higher energetic level to another, lower one to get rid of their excess energy in the form of a photon (see page 26).

RADIATION IS DANGEROUS FOR LIVING BEINGS.

MARIE CURIE

MARIE CURIE was a famous Polish scientist. She studied the phenomenon of natural radioactivity together with her husband, Pierre Curie, and they were able to identify other radioactive substances in addition to uranium: thorium, polonium, (named in honour of her country of origin, Poland) and radium.

FOR HER DISCOVERIES MARIE CURIE WON THE NOBEL PRIZE TWICE, IN 1903 AND 1911. SHE WAS THE FIRST PERSON, AND THE ONLY WOMAN, TO DO SO.

Doctors now use radiation for medical purposes. X-rays are used to see if we have a broken bone. Radiation is also used for radiation therapy, a way to treat cancer.

The discovery of radioactivity was very important because, in addition to its usefulness in medicine, it also helped us understand how matter is formed.

ATOMIC OR NUCLEAR ENERGY

Atomic energy makes it possible to create large amounts of energy from nuclear fission and fusion.

NUCLEAR FISSION

When we divide the nucleus of an atom into two, we release a lot of energy. At nuclear power stations, we use this energy to make electricity. It is also used to make atomic bombs.

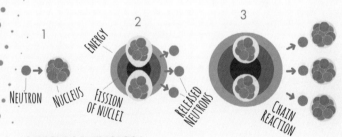

1
NEUTRON   NUCLEUS

2
ENERGY
FISSION OF NUCLEI   RELEASED NEUTRONS

3
CHAIN REACTION

NUCLEAR FUSION

When two atomic nuclei collide and join to form a bigger one, a huge amount of energy is generated. This is the source of the energy of the stars such as our SUN. Thanks to it, there is life on our planet.

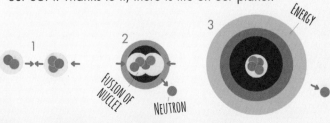

1

2
FUSION OF NUCLEI

3
ENERGY
NEUTRON

THE TUNNEL EFFECT

Can you imagine being able to travel through walls? That would be cool, wouldn't it?

Well, it turns out that particles are able to pass through barriers of energy, not too unlike our walls, and this is because of the **TUNNEL EFFECT**.

First of all, let's take an example from everyday life:

If we are listening to loud music, it can pass through a wall and be heard faintly on the other side.

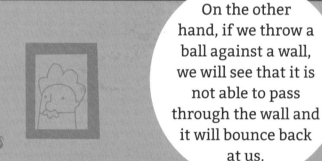

On the other hand, if we throw a ball against a wall, we will see that it is not able to pass through the wall and it will bounce back at us.

When the sound waves reach the wall of the room they bounce off it, but a small number manage to pass through and be heard faintly on the other side.

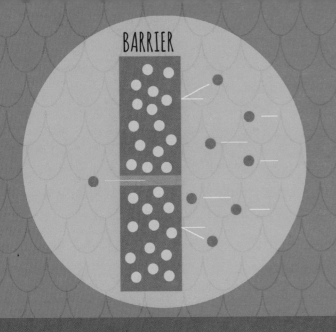

BARRIER

If you recall, an electron can behave like a PROBABILITY WAVE because of the wave–particle duality (see pages 14–15 and page 30).

When it reaches the barrier, most of the wave of the electron bounces back, but a small part has a certain chance of passing through to the other side.

When this happens, it is as if the electron has managed to cross the barrier through a TUNNEL.

This doesn't just happen with electrons, it also happens with other particles.

Since we are made up of protons, neutrons, and electrons, why can't we pass through walls?

Well, this is because the wave associated with us is so tiny that the probability of crossing a wall is very small, so small that you could wait until the end of the universe and still not find yourself on the other side. But BE CAREFUL—that doesn't mean that it can't happen.

You can give it a go, but the most likely thing is that you will spend your life banging against the wall without managing to penetrate it.

Freedom

It's getting away!

For example, in RADIOACTIVITY, the alpha particles escape from the nuclei of the atoms because of the TUNNEL EFFECT.

INSIDE THE PARTICLE ACCELERATOR AT CERN

(Conseil Européen pour la Recherche Nucléaire/European Organization for Nuclear Research)

Science pushes ahead, with theories that need to be tested through experiments. Scientists need special instruments to carry out these experiments.

And in order to study the smallest pieces of matter that we know—subatomic particles—they have built the largest instruments that have ever been made for scientists to use.

The Large Hadron Collider (LHC) is **the largest particle accelerator** in the world. Situated in a tunnel 100 meters underground near the city of Geneva, Switzerland, the accelerator forms a ring that has a 27-kilometer circumference.

Using huge magnets, the LHC accelerates **proton** beams at speeds close to the **speed of light**. The protons circulate in opposite directions inside two separate pipes until their direction is changed, and this causes them to **collide**.

The aim is **to reproduce what happened during the first moments of the universe** in order to discover how matter was formed. This includes atoms and subatomic particles, and matter that we know very little about, such as a particle called the Higgs boson, and dark matter, which makes up a quarter of the universe.

ELEMENTARY PARTICLES

ELEMENTARY PARTICLES are those that are NOT made up of smaller particles. We cannot divide them any further.

At first, it was thought that the only elementary particles that existed were those that made up the atom: the proton, the neutron, and the electron.

Thanks to particle accelerators, we now know that protons and neutrons are formed by other, smaller particles called QUARKS.

When we cause two protons to collide at great speed in a particle accelerator, they break and we can see what they have inside.

This is how we found out that the proton is formed by three quarks.

The neutron is also made up of three quarks.

NUCLEUS
QUARKS
PROTON   NEUTRON

STANDARD MODEL

This theory describes the elementary particles that we know and how they interact with each other.

Today, it is believed that there are three families of elementary particles: quarks, leptons, and bosons.

QUARKS form protons and neutrons.

MASS ≈2.4 MeV/c² CHARGE 2/3 SPIN 1/2 **u** NAME up quark	≈1.275 GeV/c² 2/3 1/2 **c** charm quark	≈172.44 GeV/c² 2/3 1/2 **t** top quark	0 0 1 **g** gluon
≈4.8 MeV/c² -1/3 1/2 **d** down quark	≈95 MeV/c² -1/3 1/2 **s** strange quark	≈4.18 GeV/c² -1/3 1/2 **b** bottom quark	0 0 1 **γ** photon
≈0.511 Mev/c² -1 1/2 **e** electron	≈105.67 MeV/c² -1 1/2 **μ** muon	≈1.7768 GeV/c² -1 1/2 **τ** tau	≈91.19 GeV/c² 0 1 **Z** Z boson
<2.2 eV/c² 0 1/2 **νe** electron neutrino	<1.7 MeV/c² 0 1/2 **νμ** muon neutrino	<15.5 MeV/c² 0 1/2 **ντ** tau neutrino	≈80.39 GeV/c² -1 1 **W** W boson

LEPTONS are the electron family.

GAUGE BOSONS are the particles that transmit force.

≈125.09 GeV/c²
0
0
H
Higgs

THE HIGGS BOSON

Not that long ago, another particle, THE HIGGS BOSON (named in honor of the person who first said that it might exist) was discovered at CERN, and it is the reason why everything has MASS.

The next time you step on the weighing scales to weigh yourself, just remember that this particle is to blame for part of your weight.

REMEMBER that each particle has its ANTIPARTICLE.

THINGS WE DO EVERY DAY USING MODERN PHYSICS

THE DISCOVERIES THAT SCIENTISTS HAVE MADE IN PHYSICS HAVE BEEN APPLIED TO MANY MODERN INVENTIONS. YOU CAN BE SURE THAT YOUR HOUSE IS FULL OF QUANTUM GADGETS.

Heat food in a MICROWAVE

The microwave's light (electromagnetic) waves cause the molecules of water in the food to vibrate. In this way they can be heated quickly and safely.

COMMUNICATE using mobile phones

Mobile devices (tablets, smartphones, laptops) are an endless source of quantum objects: touch screens, LED camera flashes, memory cards, microprocessors, the electronic circuits that they have inside, and many more objects. We also use SEMICONDUCTOR materials in all of these.

PHOTOGRAPH our insides

Thanks to X-RAYS that are able to go through us, we can see our bones and find out if we have an injury.

Boil an egg on an INDUCTION HOB

Magnetic fields cause the metal atoms of the pots and pans to vibrate and this heats them and allows us to cook.

Today, almost everything is illuminated with DIODES that emit light, in other words, LED lights. These lights consume very little energy and are made from materials known as SEMICONDUCTORS. These materials first came into use thanks to quantum physics.

Go camping with LED lights

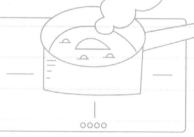

Use LASERS

In lasers, we use quantum theory to get a very narrow beam of light of a single color. Lasers have many different uses. We use them to see films on DVD, as pointers, as scalpels in operations, and even, with the most powerful ones, to cut metals.

THINGS THAT WE WILL DO SOMEDAY WITH MODERN PHYSICS

Every day science brings us closer to a part of nature that had been unknown until quite recently.

As scientists move ahead with their discoveries, we will be able to do increasingly incredible things.

Quantum computers 10 11

Our computers operate with bits; in other words, the information is built from zeros (0) and ones (1). In quantum computers we use the **qubit** (the quantum bit), which in addition to having 0 and 1 states, just like a bit, also has a combination of both, thanks to quantum physics. With qubits it is possible to process much more information, meaning that computers will be MILLIONS of times faster than those we know today.

Nanorobots

Nanorobots are made up of very few molecules and they can live in our bodies to help detect and cure illnesses.

New materials

Thanks to our knowledge of atomic structures, materials such as graphene are being developed. Graphene is very flexible and elastic; it is a hundred times more resistant than steel, very light, and one of the best conductors of electricity in existence. It will be possible to use it to construct airplanes and buildings, and we will even be able to use it to make better electronic devices and batteries that last much longer.

Teleportation

Information is already being teleported between entangled photons. In the future it will be possible to teleport large amounts of information between two points that are physically very far apart. Imagine how fast the Internet will be then!

Interactive glasses and lenses

In the future, there will be glasses where the lens itself acts as a screen, providing us with information about whatever we are looking at. And if you don't want to wear glasses, there will be contact lenses that do the same. Can you imagine sightseeing with your guide tucked inside your glasses?

Flexible screens

The screens on TVs and mobile devices will be flexible. We will be able to fold them and even roll them up. It will even be possible to have a wall covered in screen "fabric." The walls, floors or ceilings themselves will act as TV screens.

Philosophy

Quantum physics poses many questions about what **reality** is, and so in the decades to come, scientists and philosophers will have to work together to meet all the challenges that we come up with.

QUANTUM TIMELINE

1801: Young performs double-slit experiment

Einstein presents the General Theory of Relativity

1914: Start of the First World War

End of the First World War

Rutherford presents the discovery of the atomic nucleus

1910

Curie receives her first Nobel Prize for her work on radioactivity

| 1916 | 1915 | | | 1910 | 1909 | 1908 | 07 | 1906 | 1905 | 1904 |

1917

1913: Bohr publishes his atomic model

Dirac finds his equation predicting the positron, the antiparticle of the electron

Einstein publishes his four ground-breaking articles

1918

1919

De Broglie associates waves with electrons

Discovery of electron spin by Goudsmit and Uhlenbeck

1930

Chadwick discovers the neutron

1920

| 1920 | 1921 | 1922 | 1923 | 1924 | 1925 | 1926 | 19 | 928 | 1929 | 1930 | 1931 | 1932 | 1933 |

Pauli formulates the exclusion principle

Fifth Solvay Conference: Bohr and Einstein clash over quantum physics

Heisenberg announces the uncertainty principle

Schrödinger devises his thought experiment with a cat

First of Bell's inequality experiments in favor of quantum entanglement

1970

1980

1974: Feynman's double-slit thought experiment is carried out with electrons

| 1982 | 1981 | 1980 | 1979 | 1978 | 1977 | 1976 | | 1973 | 1972 | 1971 | 1970 | 1969 |

C21st

1984

Aspect experimentally verifies the hypothesis of quantum entanglement

Discovery of the bottom quark at the Fermilab in Chicago

Mid-1970s: Development of the Standard Model

First quantum teleportation at the University of Innsbruck

1985

| 1986 | 1987 | 1988 | 1989 | 1990 | 1991 | 1992 | 1993 | 1994 | 1995 | 1996 | 1997 | 1998 | 1999 | 20 |

1990

1850

1860

1864: Maxwell presents his equations on electromagnetism

1870

1861: Maxwell puts forward wave theory of light

C20th

1897: Thompson discovers the electron

1895: Röntgen discovers the X-ray

1890

1879: Birth of Einstein

1880

1900

k theorizes ergy quanta

1896: Becquerel discovers radioactivity

Development of the Manhattan Project for the US construction of nuclear weapons

The first atomic bombs are dropped on the cities of Hiroshima and Nagasaki. End of the Second World War

1940

1950

6 | 1937 | 1938 | ☠ | 1940 | 1941 | 1942 | 1943 | 1944 | 1945 | 1946 | 1947 | 1948 | 1949 | 1950 | 1951 | 1952 | 1953

Start of the Second World War

Foundation of CERN (European Organization for Nuclear Research)

First civil nuclear power plant in Obninsk, Russia

Bell proposes his inequality rule and refutes Von Neumann

1960

Development of the first microchip

7 | 1966 | 1965 | 64 | 1963 | 1962 | 1961 | 1960 | 1959 | 1958 | 1957 | 1956 | 1955 | 1954

Discovery of the up quark at the SLAC (National Accelerator Laboratory, USA)

Quark model developed (Gell-Mann finds the word in a book by James Joyce)

Construction of the first laser

The Higgs boson particle is detected at CERN

Error-free transfer of data by quantum teleportation, a crucial step in the move toward the quantum Internet

Development of the first quantum computers

2002 | 2003 | 2004 | 2005 | 2006 | 2007 | 2008 | 2009 | 2010 | 2011 | 2012 | 2013 | 2014 | 2015 | 2016 | 2017 | 2018 | 20

2010

A MATHEMATICAL UNIVERSE

All the scientific ideas that have been explained in this book with words can be expressed using another language, that of mathematics. MATHEMATICS is the language of the UNIVERSE and we have had to learn it in order to understand the REALITY that surrounds us.

Here are some famous mathematical equations

Newton's Second Law

$$\vec{F} = m\vec{a}$$

This law describes the cause of the momentum of objects. When we wish to change the momentum of an object, we have to apply a force to it; otherwise it will remain as it was.

Maxwell's Equations

$$\nabla \vec{E} = \frac{\rho}{\epsilon_0}$$

$$\nabla \times \vec{E} = -\frac{\partial \vec{B}}{\partial t}$$

$$\nabla \vec{B} = 0$$

$$\nabla \times \vec{B} = \mu_0 \vec{J} + \frac{1}{c^2}\frac{\partial \vec{E}}{\partial t}$$

These describe electromagnetic phenomena. They show us that light is formed by electromagnetic waves that travel at the speed of light.

Wave-particle Duality

The Schrödinger Equation (time-independent)

$$E|\Psi\rangle = \hat{H}|\Psi\rangle$$

This equation is used to calculate the orbitals of atoms and molecules. Electrons can be found in these.

Heisenberg's Uncertainty Principle

$$\Delta x \Delta p \geq \frac{\hbar}{2}$$

If we are very sure of the position of a particle, we cannot precisely know its momentum, and vice versa.

$$\lambda = \frac{h}{p}$$

The de Broglie Equation

This equation shows us that matter can also behave like a wave.

Source: Wikipedia. Einstein 1921 by F. Schmutzer

Energy of the Photon

$$E = h\nu$$

This is the equation Planck found for quanta of energy, which Einstein then used later on to explain the photoelectric effect.

Mass–Energy Equivalence (Einstein)

This is where the energy of the Sun comes from.

$$E = mc^2$$

Dirac's Equation

Thanks to this equation, we learned of the existence of antimatter.

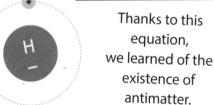

$$(i\hbar\gamma^\mu\partial_\mu - mc)\psi = 0$$

Universal Constants

These are numbers that appear in mathematical equations that never change. They are always the same. Here are three of the most important physical constants:

Plank's Constant:

$$h = 6.62607015 \times 10^{-34} \text{ Js}$$

Speed of Light:

$$c = 299\ 792\ 458 \text{ m/s}$$

Elementary Charge (or charge of the electron):

$$e = 1.60217662 \times 10^{-19} \text{ C}$$

ACKNOWLEDGMENTS

Sheddad Thanks to **Diego Jurado** and **Carles Muñoz**, who share my passion for physics, for proofreading the book [Spanish edition]; also **Salva Sanchis,** for contributing with his vision as a father, artist, and friend. To my wife **Helena** for the revision and correction of the text and, especially, for always being there; and to our two children, **Tarek** and **Unai**, for having been the inspiration for this book. And, of course, to **Inma**. Without them, nothing would make sense.

Eduard Many thanks to the people who have made this book possible, especially to **Meli**, but also to **Pere**, **Lourdes,** and **Ariadna**, for their constant support and infinite patience. Also to my beta-testers, **Xavi Villanueva**, **Josep Boix**, **Pere Altarriba,** and **Picu Oms**, who have been kind enough to see what we could not see any more.

And to Albert Einstein, Max Planck, Niels Bohr, Marie Curie... and all the men and women dedicated to science whose work has and will make it possible to advance further and further.

ALSO AVAILABLE

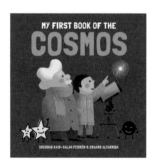

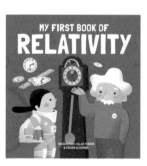

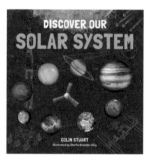

My First Book of the Cosmos
978-1-78708-077-5

My First Book of Relativity
978-1-78708-033-1

Discover our Solar System
978-1-78708-017-1

First published 2018 in English by Button Books, an imprint of Guild of Master Craftsman Publications Ltd, Castle Place, 166 High Street, Lewes, East Sussex BN7 1XU, UK. Reprinted 2019, 2021, 2022. © Sheddad Kaid-Salah Ferrón and Eduard Altarriba, 2017. English text © GMC Publications Ltd, 2018. ISBN 978 1 78708 013 3. Distributed in the United States by Publishers Group West. All rights reserved. This translation of *My First Book of Quantum Physics* is published by arrangement with Alababala. The right of Sheddad Kaid-Salah Ferrón and Eduard Altarriba to be identified as the authors of this work has been asserted in accordance with the Copyright, Designs, and Patents Act 1988, sections 77 and 78. No part of this publication may be reproduced, stored in a retrieval system, or transmitted in any form or by any means without the prior permission of the publisher and copyright owner. While every effort has been made to obtain permission from the copyright holders for all material used in this book, the publishers will be pleased to hear from anyone who has not been appropriately acknowledged and to make the correction in future reprints. The publishers and authors can accept no legal responsibility for any consequences arising from the application of information, advice, or instructions given in this publication. A catalog record for this book is available from the British Library. Publisher: Jonathan Bailey. Production Director: Jim Bulley. Senior Project Editor: Sara Harper. Managing Art Editor: Gilda Pacitti. Technical Consultants: Martin Bradley, Mike Brown, and Miles Radford. Americanizer: Tammy Graves. Color origination by GMC Reprographics. Printed and bound in China.

Button Books

FSC
MIX
Paper
FSC® C020056

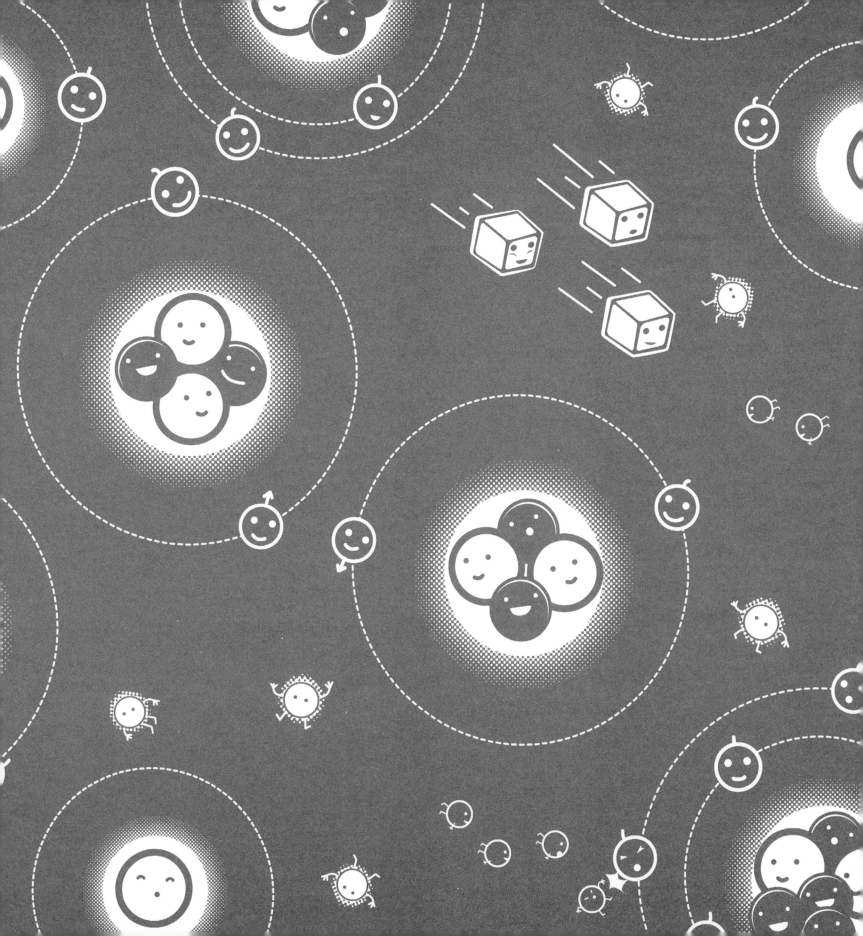